I0797617

HORSE BREEDS

ARABIAN

BY WHITNEY SANDERSON

Kids Core
An Imprint of Abdo Publishing
abdobooks.com

abdobooks.com

Published by Abdo Publishing, a division of ABDO, PO Box 398166, Minneapolis, Minnesota 55439.

Printed in the United States of America, North Mankato, Minnesota.
052025
092025

Cover Photo: Makarova Viktoria/Shutterstock Images
Interior Photos: ClarkandCompany/E+/Getty Images, 4–5; Daniel Lozano Gonzalez/Moment/Getty Images, 7; Shutterstock Images, 8, 14; Slawik, C./juniors@wildlife/Juniors Bildarchiv GmbH/Alamy, 10–11; Red Line Editorial, 12; C. Slawik/Juniors Bildarchiv GmbH/Alamy, 13; Thomas Warnack/picture-alliance/dpa/AP Images, 16; Noushad Thekkayil/NurPhoto/Getty Images, 18; iStockphoto, 20–21; Six_Characters/E+/Getty Images, 23; Lokibaho/E+/Getty Images, 24; B. David Cathell/Alamy, 26; Alexia Khruscheva/Shutterstock Images, 28–29

Editor: Marie Pearson
Series Designer: Ryan Gale

Library of Congress Control Number: 2024949005

Publisher's Cataloging-in-Publication Data

Names: Sanderson, Whitney, author.
Title: Arabian / by Whitney Sanderson
Description: Minneapolis, Minnesota: Abdo Publishing, 2026 | Series: Horse breeds | Includes online resources and index.
Identifiers: ISBN 9781098297497 (lib. bdg.) | ISBN 9798384930013 (ebook)
Subjects: LCSH: Arabian horse--Juvenile literature. | Horses--Juvenile literature. | Horse breeds--Juvenile literature. | Zoology--Juvenile literature.
Classification: DDC 636.11--dc23

CONTENTS

Arabians are athletic and can be used for many other activities besides endurance racing.

CHAPTER 1

THE ARABIAN SPIRIT

Lily stopped Emir at the base of the mountain slope. What was the safest path up? The Arabian horse's delicate ears pointed forward. He was also looking for the best way up.

Emir picked his way through the rocks and bushes. Lily leaned forward to help him balance. The path became very steep. It felt like they were climbing into the sky.

Emir's powerful hind legs pushed them upward. He snorted with each stride. With one last surge, they were back on level ground. They had reached the top!

Lily slowed Emir to a walk to let him rest. But he pranced eagerly. He wanted to go faster.

An Arabian Tale

In 1941, Walter Farley wrote a book about a boy and an Arabian stallion, a male horse that can reproduce, who are shipwrecked on a desert island. The book is called *The Black Stallion*. It later became a series of books and a popular movie.

Wetting down horses helps keep them from getting too hot when exercising.

Lily let him. With his quick, light strides, it felt like he could go all day. And he would have to do just that for this endurance ride. They would be traveling 50 miles (80 km) today!

Lily saw people and horses gathered at a vet check ahead. She **dismounted**. Her mother, who had come to help, gave Emir a drink. Lily sponged cool water over his neck and chest.

Like other horses, Arabians are social and should be kept with at least one other horse.

A veterinarian checked Emir's heart rate. She made sure he was not limping. "He's in great shape," said the vet. "You can keep going."

Lily was relieved. Endurance rides are tough. Just finishing one would be a big success. She mounted again. Emir was eager to go. They would face rough trails and water crossings. But Lily knew that she and her brave Arabian horse could take them on together.

Desert Born

The Arabian is one of the oldest horse breeds. It originated in the deserts of the Middle East. From there, people brought Arabians all over the world.

There are more than 1 million Arabian horses in the United States and Canada. Many more live in other countries. People love Arabians for their endurance and beauty.

Further Evidence

Watch this video about endurance riding below. Does it give any new evidence to support Chapter One?

Distance Riding

abdocorelibrary.com/arabian

Arabians needed to be able to travel far in harsh desert conditions.

CHAPTER 2

HISTORY OF THE ARABIAN

About 4,500 years ago, Bedouin people began breeding horses. They lived in the Arabian **Peninsula**, a desert area in the Middle East. These horses were important to the Bedouin people.

Arabian Peninsula Map

The Arabian Peninsula is now home to several countries, including Saudi Arabia, Yemen, Oman, and the United Arab Emirates.

Bedouins are nomadic. They do not stay in one place but move with the seasons. Bedouins have long used their horses for carrying supplies. Their horses needed endurance, or

Bedouins bred their horses to be gentle. Some Bedouins still breed Arabians.

the ability to travel long distances without getting tired. They needed to do well in the daytime heat.

The horses were used during battles and **raids**. Bedouins often rode mares, or female horses, during raids. Stallions whinny when they see other horses, but mares do not. Bedouin people treated their horses like family. They let the horses sleep in their tents to protect them from thieves and cold desert nights.

Some people in Saudi Arabia dress their Arabian horses and themselves in traditional outfits to honor their history.

The Bedouin horses became the breed known as the Arabian. Kings in the Middle East sometimes gave Arabian horses as gifts to rulers of other countries. The breed began to spread through the world.

Arabians around the World

War also brought Arabian horses to Europe. Between the 1000s and 1200s, Christians from Europe and Muslims from the Middle East had wars called the Crusades. They fought for control of land near the city of Jerusalem in what is now Israel.

Europeans had large, powerful horses bred to hold knights wearing heavy armor. But Europeans saw people from the Middle East riding Arabian horses in battles during the Crusades. The Arabians were fast. Over time, people in Europe stopped wearing armor, which offered little protection against guns. They crossed their larger, heavier horses with Arabians to make their horses faster.

Some people today have farms where they breed Arabian horses.

Arabians were used to make Thoroughbreds, American quarter horses, and other popular breeds. Some countries kept breeding purebred Arabians. Egypt, England, Russia, and Poland became especially known for their fine Arabian horses.

In 1893, the **sultan** of Turkey sent 45 Arabian horses to the world's fair in Chicago, Illinois. People were impressed by their speed and good looks. Many famous and wealthy people in the United States wanted Arabian horses of their own!

A Daring Rescue

During World War II (1939–1945), US Army soldiers rescued 22 Polish Arabian horses from the invading German Nazis. The Nazis wanted to breed the horses, but Colonel Hank Reed of the US Army didn't want them to fall into enemy hands. After the rescue, some of the Arabians came to live in the United States.

Arabian horse registries hold shows where the horses are judged on how closely they match the breed's ideal look.

The first Arabian horse registry in the United States began in 1908. Its purpose was to keep records of all Arabian horses. Today, it is called the Arabian Horse Association.

A Bedouin legend says that Allah, the god of Islam, created the Arabian horse from the south wind, saying:

> I create thee, oh Arabian. To thy **forelock**, I bind victory in battle. . . . I establish thee as one of the glories of the Earth. . . . I give thee flight without wings.

Source: Mary Oommen. “The Majestic Arabian: Celebrated in Poetry, Immortalised in Myth.” *Oman Observer*, 3 Nov. 2018, omanobserver.com. Accessed 18 Oct. 2024.

What’s the Big Idea?

Read this quote carefully. What is the main idea? Explain how the main idea is supported by details.

Arabians are finely built and athletic.

CHAPTER 3

LIVING WITH THE ARABIAN

Spirited and graceful, Arabian horses are easy to recognize. They have dished, or slightly inward-curving, faces with small, pointed ears. They have arched necks and short backs. These horses carry their tails high.

Arabians usually stand between 14 and 15.2 hands tall. A hand is 4 inches (10 cm). Arabians weigh between 900 and 1,100 pounds (410 and 500 kg). They can be black, **chestnut**, **bay**, gray, or **roan**. Their skin is black to protect them from the sun.

Arabians are smart and friendly horses. They love their owners. Some Arabians bred for showing can have fiery tempers. Other Arabians are gentle. Children can ride them.

Endurance and Beauty

Arabians shine in endurance riding. Horses and riders cover long distances. The Tevis Cup is a famous endurance race. It happens in the Sierra Nevada mountains in California.

Some Arabians are ridden in English discipline, which features a light saddle and putting pressure on the reins to direct the horse.

Western riders use large saddles and can touch a rein against the horse's neck to turn it.

Horses and riders have 24 hours to travel 100 miles (161 km). Most of the horses who have won the Tevis Cup are Arabians.

There are also shows for Arabian horses. The largest Arabian horse show in the United States is in Scottsdale, Arizona. Horses can compete in English, Western, and **driving** events. There are also events for Arabian costumes.

In halter classes, handlers lead the horses. Judges look at each part of the horse's body and how it moves. They look for a short back, a deep chest, strong legs, and a fine head. Arabian horses are light on their feet. They often seem to float across the ground.

A Royal Arabian

One of the most famous Arabian horses is Marwan Al Shaqab. He is owned by the royal family of Qatar, a country in the Middle East. He won the World Champion title for Arabian stallions three times. He has more than 1,000 foals!

Costume competitions include elements of traditional clothing from the Arabian Peninsula.

Arabian horses can be very valuable. In 2017, an Arabian filly named Om El Erodite sold at an auction in Arizona for $1.5 million! It is easy to see why the Arabian horse spread far beyond its desert home. This ancient breed has inspired people around the world with its beauty and spirit.

Explore Online

Visit the website below. Does it give any new information about Arabian activities that wasn't in Chapter Three?

Arabian Horse Disciplines

abdocorelibrary.com/arabian

BREED TRAITS

Short back

High-set tail

Long, arched neck
Dished face
Large, dark eyes
Large nostrils

Glossary

bay
brown with a black mane and tail

chestnut
a solid brown color, ranging from golden to dark brown

dismounted
got down from a horse's back

driving
a sport where a horse pulls a cart or carriage

forelock
the part of a horse's mane that falls between its ears

peninsula
a piece of land sticking out into the water

raids
surprise attacks to take goods or animals

roan
a color with white and dark hairs mixed together

sultan
a king or ruler

Online Resources

To learn more about Arabians and other horses, visit our free resource websites below.

Visit **abdocorelibrary.com** or scan this QR code for free Common Core resources for teachers and students, including vetted activities, multimedia, and booklinks, for deeper subject comprehension.

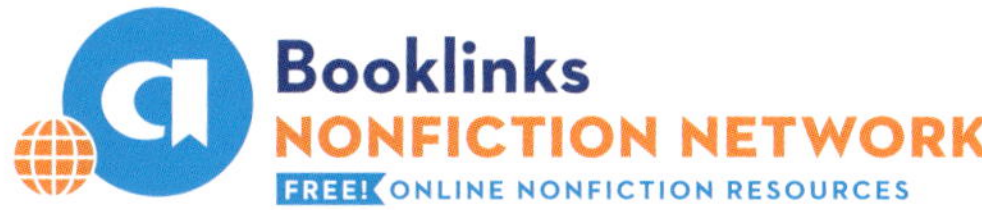

Visit **abdobooklinks.com** or scan this QR code for free additional online weblinks for further learning. These links are routinely monitored and updated to provide the most current information available.

Learn More

Cavanaugh, Neil. *Can't Get Enough Horse Stuff.* National Geographic, 2023.

Mazzarella, Kerri. *Arabian.* Crabtree, 2024.

Ventura, Marne. *Horses.* Abdo, 2023.

Index

About the Author

Whitney Sanderson grew up riding horses as a member of a 4-H club and competing in local horse shows. She is the author of numerous children's books.